# The Sport of Politics Simplified

# Democrats versus Republicans

# The 2016 Spectator's Guide

## By

## R. L. Snyder

The Sport of Politics Simplified
Democrats versus Republicans
The 2016 Spectator's Guide
By R. L. Snyder
Copyright © 2016
All Rights Reserved

ISBN-13: 978-1537424668

# Table of Contents

## Introduction

Politics is a sport where the objective of the game is to capture your vote. Instead of using athleticism, politicians use intellect, strategy, advertising, public relations, the media and words strung together to persuade you to vote for them. So to truly make your vote count, you have to understand the competitors and teams playing the game, their goals, and your role in determining the winners of the game.

## Competitors

The sport of politics in the United States at the national level in 2016 is made up of two major teams that compete against each other for your vote: Democrats and Republicans.

Democrats are also known as liberals or progressives. Their mascot is a donkey. Their team color is blue.

Republicans are also known as conservatives or GOP (Grand Old Party). Their mascot is an elephant. Their team color is red.

Each team selects players that have similar beliefs. (What those beliefs are will be discussed later.) The team that captures the most votes controls a division of government.

## Divisions of Government

Democrats and Republicans compete for your vote in order to obtain control of the three main divisions of government. The three divisions are the Legislative, President, and Judicial.

You can vote directly for players in the Legislative and President divisions. You cannot vote directly for the players in the Judicial division because those players are selected by the winner of the President division.

## 1) **President Division**

Only one player, either a Democrat or a Republican, can win the President division. If the player wins, he or she is then called the "president" and gets a four-year contract at $400,000 a year.

## 2) **Legislative Division**

The legislative division is made up of two conferences: the House (short for House of Representatives) and the Senate.

### **House of Representatives**

435 players from our 50 united states make up the House. The number of players is determined by each state's population. The larger the population, the more players the teams can obtain. You get to vote for only one player in your state. Who you get to vote for is based on where you live in your state. The player that collects the most votes wins, is then called a "rep" (short for representative), and gets a two-year contract at $174,000 a year. The leader of the House gets $223,500 per year.

### **Senate**

100 players from our 50 united states make up the Senate. Each state is allowed only two players. You get to vote only for

players in your state. The player that collects the most votes wins, is then called a "senator," and gets a six-year contract at $174,000 a year. The leaders of the senate get $193,400 a year.

## Congress

Congress is the House of Representatives and the Senate.

## Objective of the Teams

In the President Division, the objective of each team is for one of their players to become president. The current president is Democrat Barack Obama. His contract expires in January 2017 and must retire after that. You get to vote in November 2016 to determine who gets to play president for the next four years.

As of September 2016, the Democrat nominee for president is Hillary Rodham Clinton. The Republican nominee for president is Donald J. Trump. Both teams and their supporters will spend billions of US dollars to persuade you to vote for their player.

In the House, the objective of each team is to capture 218 reps, which is the minimum to obtain a majority (435 divided by 2, plus 1 gives you 218). If they do, the other team can do nothing to stop the laws they want to pass. Currently, the Republicans have 247 reps and the Democrats have 186 reps. Two reps are vacant. You'll hear a lot of complaining from Democrats in the House because they cannot pass their laws without Republican cooperation. The contract of every rep on both teams in the House expires this year. Most of the current reps want to play for another two years. Again, you get to vote to determine which rep gets to play. Both teams, players and their supporters will spend millions of US dollars to persuade you to vote for their side.

In the Senate, the objective of each team is to obtain 51 senators, but if a team gets 60, the other team could do nothing to stop them from passing their laws. However, the team that gets more than 50 senators will control which laws are brought up for a vote. Currently, the Republicans control the Senate with 54 senators while the Democrats have 46. (The rules as to how the Senate works are kind of complicated, so since you are a spectator I won't attempt to explain its workings.) But since neither team currently has 60 senators, for the most part each team can stop the other from passing their laws. But if one team can obtain 60 votes, a law can be voted on and passed if 51 senators agree. You'll hear a lot of complaining from both Democrats and Republicans senators because they cannot pass their laws without some cooperation from the other team.

In 2016, 34 of the 100 senators are up for election in November. Of those 34 senators, 24 are Republicans and 12 are Democrats. If either of your state's two senators has a contract expiring this year (or chooses not to play again), you get to vote to determine which senator gets to play. And again, both teams, players and their supporters will spend millions of US dollars to persuade you to vote for their side.

As you can see by looking at the objectives of the teams, the team that can win the majority of players gets to rule. Thus, majority rules!

## Passing Laws (In simplistic terms)

To pass federal laws, at least 218 players from the House of Representatives and 51 from the Senate have to agree to pass any law that originated in the House or Senate. If both the House and Senate agree to pass a law, it only becomes a federal law if the President also agrees to pass that law.

## Divided Government – Congress and President

When neither team controls the House, Senate, and President at the same time, divided government occurs. What divided government really means is either the law-making process slows down or doesn't happen at all. (You might hear the terms gridlock and partisanship. These terms mean the same as divided government.) This is the current situation in Washington, D.C. And just like in other sports where a team has no intention of helping the other team win, Democrats and Republicans have no desire to help the other team in passing their laws. Therefore, both Democrats and Republicans desire complete control of the House, Senate, and President in order to pass their laws without opposition from the other team. From now until the election in November 2016, both teams and their supporters will do everything lawful (and truthful?) to persuade you to vote for their players. That puts all the power in your hands. Your vote is very important to both teams.

As a side note, you might hear the words partisanship and bipartisanship used during this election year. Partisanship is where neither team cooperates with the other; bipartisanship is where they do cooperate with each other. Believe it or not, sometimes bipartisanship occurs. National security and national emergencies are a couple areas where the teams usually cooperate. But most of the time, the two teams do not agree on how to solve most issues facing the country.

## Divided Government – Judicial

Since divided government between Congress and the President currently exists, the President's ability to appoint judges has become extremely important. More and more laws are being implemented by activist judges at all levels of the Judicial Division. This is another reason why who gets elected president is very important.

## How You Should Vote

Now that you understand how politics is a sport, you have to decide how to vote for the players. Since the game is all about numbers and getting a majority of players to win for the team, let's take a quick look again at the objectives of each team.

Both teams want their player to become the president.

Both teams want to win at least 218 players in the House and 51 in the Senate. If neither team wins all three divisions of government, the following will occur: No meaningful laws will be passed over the next two years unless a national crisis occurs or the citizens revolt, divided government will rule, and the major issues facing this country will not be solved through legislation.

At the national level, you get to vote at least once and possibly two times in November 2016 depending on where you live. One vote is for your House rep. The second vote is for your Senator is one is up for election in your state.

Politics is personal. What's good for you is good for the country. When you vote, take the attitude that nobody else is voting and only your vote will determine the winners. You want government to pass laws that will make your life better, your children's future brighter, and the country stronger. So it only makes sense to vote for players on the same team. Therefore, when you vote, vote for either all Democrat or all Republican players. The team needs a majority of players to get laws passed.

So which team and their respective players should you vote for? To answer that question you have to decide the most important issue or issues you believe needs to solve and what team has the best approach in solving the problem. Remember, the players on each team are on that team because they have similar beliefs on how to solve our country's important issues.

Because they have similar beliefs, they will be reluctant to assist the other team in passing laws. For the most part, the teams seldom agree on how to solve the important issues facing our country. The important issues and how the Democrats and Republicans would solve them will be presented later.

## Campaign 2016

Once you've determined the most important issue or issues facing this country and the team you believe can best solve that problem, you can simply tune out all the rest of the political campaigning, such as newscasts, discussions, advertisements, debates, and even television and radio talk shows, that will take place up to the November 2016 elections.

The goal of the teams and players is to win your vote. Players and their supporters will attempt to persuade you to vote for them and not their opponent. To do so, you will be bombarded with political advertising on television, radio, news print, and the internet. You might also receive unsolicited political mail and telephone calls. Players and their supporters may visit your home, or you may encounter them in public places. The whole political campaign process will get down right nasty. Insults, dirty tricks, slanderous rumors, criticism, border-line truths, and negativity will rule. Many voters will become so disgusted with the campaign process that they will not even vote. And those that don't vote will be eliminated from deciding which players and teams will win this game. So ignore all those distractions because you're not voting for homecoming queen or prom king. It's not important if a player is a great or poor debater, has style and grace, is likeable, wealthy, or doesn't live like you do. A player's religion or skin color won't affect your life after the election. It's unlikely that you'll ever see, yet alone meet, a political candidate in person. So tune out all that political campaign gibberish because the only thing that's important is the team - either the Democrats or Republicans - you've chosen to solve our country's problems. And once you've chosen the team, vote for their respective players at the national, state, and local levels. If you do, your votes won't be wasted because it's a game of mathematics where the majority rules. It's that simple. You will help decide the winner of this game!

## Democrats versus Republicans – The Differences

If you're undecided as to which team to vote for, decide which issue (or issues) facing our country is the most important to you. Once you determine that, decide which team has the best approach to solving that problem. To assist you in your decisions, the following are the most common issues facing our country today and how the Democrats and Republicans would attempt to solve them. Remember, though there are sometimes exception to this rule, the players on each team overwhelmingly vote together as a team on most of these issues.

After reading through the following issues, you might discover that you disagree with what each team supports and opposes. You may become frustrated that neither team completely agrees with all of your views. So what! Politics is messy. No team is perfect and neither is life. Pick the issue or issues most important to you and the team that has the best solution to make your world better! Good luck.

To identify the differences, voting records, campaign literature, TV and radio programs, newspaper and magazine articles, and the internet were used.

## 1) Growing The Economy and Jobs

This issue is probably the most important in 2016 because obtaining employment is a major concern while economic growth is stagnant. Americans want to see their standard of living increase.

Democrats support raising taxes on wealthy American citizens and spending more taxpayer money on federal jobs training programs, fixing existing roadways or building new ones, improving or developing new sources of energy such as wind and solar, modernizing classrooms and schools, and expanding the health care industry to meet the new government requirements. Democrats believe government policies can grow the economy and create jobs.

Republicans support reducing or eliminating wasteful government spending and burdensome regulations and taxes on businesses. They'd also increase exploration of current energy sources such as oil and natural gas within the United States and off its shores, and expand free trade with other countries. Republicans believe that the creativity, initiative, resources, and knowledge of private businesses will grow the economy and create jobs.

## 2) **The Government Deficit**

The government deficit is the dollar amount annual government spending exceeds annual government revenue. In 2010, government spending exceeded government revenue by $1.29 trillion. In 2013 it was $680 billion. The Congressional Budget Office estimates that the government deficit will be approximately $350 billion a year for the next ten years.

Democrats believe government spending should not be reduced but revenue increased by taxing wealthy Americans.

Republicans believe wasteful government spending should be reduced and revenue increased by building a more pro-business environment.

## 3) **The Government Debt**

The government debt is the sum of the government deficits since the government was founded.

Democrats and Republicans can't agree on how to reduce the government debt because they can't agree on how to reduce the government deficit. The debt will continue to grow until government revenues exceed government spending, which doesn't seem likely to occur any time soon!

## 4) <u>Raising the Debt Ceiling or Debt Limit</u>

The amount of debt the federal government is allowed to have is set by Congress and is currently over $19 trillion. If spending continues to exceed revenues, by law the ceiling must be raised in order for the government to pay its bills. If the ceiling isn't raised, the government shuts down.

Democrats support raising the debt limit because the current recession has forced spending to exceed revenue and the government must continue to operate to provide services to the citizens. They favor raising revenue via raising taxes.

Republicans oppose raising the debt limit because no country's economy can survive if government spending continues to exceed revenues year after year. However, they would agree to raise the debt ceiling only if equal or greater spending cuts were made.

## 5) <u>Political Earmarks</u>

A political earmark is where a politician spends taxpayer money on a specific project for the benefit of a constituent or constituents. It is also known as pork-barrel, special interest, or wasteful spending.

Democrats support political earmarks because it is a great way to thank their constituents for their political and financial support.

Republicans oppose political earmarks because they

believe earmarks are inappropriate at a time when the government is running a huge financial deficit.

## 6) **Pay As You Go (PAYGO)**

PAYGO is a procedure where every dollar spent must be paid for by either raising taxes or cutting other spending. Conversely, every dollar received from tax cuts must be paid for by either cutting spending or raising other taxes. The intent is to prevent budget deficits.

Democrats support PAYGO as long as taxes are raised and no government spending cut.

Republicans support PAYGO as long as wasteful government spending is cut and no taxes are raised.

## 7) **Balanced Budget Amendment**

A Balanced Budget Amendment would force government spending to equal government revenue. Our federal government doesn't have to balance its budget, but the 50 states do.

Democrats oppose a Balance Budget Amendment because the spending cuts would be too painful for Americans to accept.

Republicans support a Balanced Budget Amendment because it's probably the only way to force the government to 'live within their means' by forcing spending to equal revenue.

## 8) <u>Freezing Federal Employees Pay</u>

Democrats believe that federal employees pay should not be frozen in order to save government money.

Republicans support freezing federal employees pay because it saves government money. Plus, they believe government employees are overpaid and have more generous benefits compared to similar jobs in the private sector.

## 9) <u>Increasing the Minimum Wage and a Living Wage</u>

Minimum wage is the lowest hourly wage an employer must pay an employee. The federal minimum wage is set by Congress and is currently $7.25 per hour. But states and cities can set their hourly minimum wage higher, and many have a higher minimum wage than the federal minimum wage. A living wage is the hourly pay necessary to live and survive in a particular city because the cost of living can vary from city to city. A living wage only applies to cities and is higher than the federal minimum wage.

Democrats support raising the federal minimum wage and living wages in expensive cities because hourly wage increases have not kept up with the cost of living and surviving.

Republicans oppose raising the federal minimum wage and living wages in expensive cities because it increases labor costs on businesses. And those affected businesses will either pass that additional cost onto consumers or lay off employees.

## 10) <u>Austerity</u>

Austerity is a policy where government spending is severely reduced in order to get the government's fiscal house in order and avoid national bankruptcy. Austerity policies have been implemented in European countries to reduce their deficits and debt, resulting in many public riots and additional hardships on the citizens.

Democrats support increasing government spending, not cutting it, because they believe spending will create jobs and stimulate an economic recovery. Plus, government spending cuts will increase unemployment and the deficit because the government will have to pay unemployment benefits and other benefits if the unemployed cannot find new jobs. They support delaying any government spending cuts as long as possible and focusing on growth instead.

Republicans support cutting government spending because there is a lot of wasteful spending and believe the United States is headed towards a similar financial situation experienced by some European countries. Plus, they believe increasing government spending will only dig us into a deeper financial hole. They support cutting government spending immediately because the longer it is delayed the more difficult it will be to solve later.

Republicans use this analogy: When a typical American household goes into debt, they cut spending, not increase it.

They believe our government should behave the same way.

## 11) <u>Federal Income Taxes</u>

Democrats support increasing federal income taxes on wage earners making $200,000 or more.

Republicans oppose increasing federal income taxes on any wage earners. Many of those making over $200,000 are small businesses owners, and most new jobs are created by small businesses. They believe wasteful government spending should be cut first before raising taxes is even considered.

The Democrats and Republicans actually compromised on this issue. Individuals earning over $400,000 a year pay the highest tax rate.

## 12) <u>Tax Cuts For The Wealthy</u>

Democrats support tax cuts for everyone but the wealthy. They believe wealthy Americans pay too little in taxes.

Republicans support tax cuts for everyone, including the wealthy.

## 13) <u>Buffett Rule</u>

The Buffett Rule, named after billionaire investor Warren Buffet, is a proposal that any American citizen that earns a minimum of $1 million a year pay a minimum 30% income tax on those earnings.

Democrats support the Buffett Rule. They believe

wealthy Americans should pay higher taxes to pay for government spending.

Republicans oppose the Buffett Rule. They oppose higher taxes on all American wage earners. They believe that wasteful government spending should be eliminated before any tax increase.

## 14) Flat Income Tax Rate

Democrats oppose a flat income tax rate because it raises tax rates on low-wage earners. Plus, they believe in taxing high-wage earners more than low-wage earners because high-wage earners can afford to pay the additional taxes.

Republicans support a flat income tax rate because it is fair for all wage earners and doesn't discriminate against high-wage earners.

## 15) Value-Added Tax

A value-added tax is tax that makes products and services more expensive for consumers. It is being discussed as an additional government revenue source.

Democrats support a value-added tax because the government will collect more revenue on every consumer purchase of a product or service.

Republicans oppose a value-added tax because it raises the cost of products and services to manufacturers, retailers, and consumers.

## 16) <u>Corporate Income Taxes</u>

Democrats believe that corporate income taxes should be increased and loopholes closed because many large corporations pay very little in taxes compared to the profits they earn.

Republicans believe corporate income taxes should be reduced so businesses can grow, hire additional employees, and compete with foreign corporations in countries with lower tax rates than ours.

## 17) <u>Corporate Tax Breaks For Sending Jobs Overseas</u>

Businesses currently can obtain a tax break via a tax deduction if they close plants in the United States and move them out of the United States.

Democrats oppose this law because corporations shouldn't be rewarded for shipping jobs elsewhere when the unemployment rate is so high in the United States.

Republicans support this law because businesses have to compete globally and this tax break reduces corporate relocation expenses.

## 18) <u>Corporate Welfare</u>

Corporate welfare is where our government gives financial assistance to businesses.

Democrats want to increase taxes on corporations to help pay for government spending. They believe corporations are not paying their fair share and enjoy too many tax breaks.

Republicans believe corporations need all the assistance they can get in a very competitive global economy because growth, new jobs, and government revenue sources will only come from businesses.

## 19) Tax Loopholes

Tax loopholes are laws that allow people and businesses to pay lower taxes.

Democrats oppose tax loopholes because more government revenue is needed to pay for government spending.

Republicans support tax loopholes because they help citizens and businesses.

## 20) Consumer Protection

Democrats support tougher regulations to protect consumers from unfair practices and products.

Republicans usually oppose consumer protection regulations because these unfair practices and products are very profitable to businesses.

## 21) Derivatives / Credit Default Swaps

Derivatives and credit default swaps are investments that helped cause the banking crisis and recent recession. These investments are complex, secret, profitable, very risky and involve billions of dollars.

Democrats support making these investments less secret

and open to oversight by government regulators because the collapse of these investments would severely hurt the world economy and financial system.

Republicans oppose tougher regulation of these investments because they are extremely profitable for businesses.

## 22) **Bank Bailouts**

Democrats and Republicans voted to save the financial banking system by providing banks with billions of taxpayer dollars. Both teams will bail out US banks in the future in order to stabilize the financial system and prevent investor panic.

## 23) **Banks That Are Too Big To Fail**

Democrats support breaking up the largest banks because they don't want the failure of a large bank to threaten our entire financial system again.

Republicans oppose breaking up the largest banks because they are necessary to compete against large foreign banks.

## 24) **State-Owned Banks**

State-owned banks are banks owned by the government. They provide loans that private or commercial banks typically would not make.

Democrats support state-owned banks because they can decide who receives a loan. They believe private banks discriminate and do not usually loan money to small and medium-size high-risk ventures.

Republicans oppose state-owned banks because they believe the private sector/free market, not political bureaucrats, should determine who receives loans. Plus, the tax payers' money is at risk if a loan defaults.

### 25) Class Warfare

Democrats support class warfare because they believe it appeals to those that are not wealthy and will most likely vote for Democrats.

Republicans oppose class warfare because they believe we should be unified as Americans, not segregated by wealth for political purposes.

### 26) Income Inequality

Income inequality means some people earn a lot more money than others.

Democrats believe income inequality is increasing. They want to put more money into the pockets of those with low income. To do this, they want to raise the federal minimum wage, extend unemployment benefits and increase taxes on high income individuals.

Republicans believe income inequality is acceptable because some individuals earn more income due to their talent, experience, education and effort. To redistribute income is a disincentive for success. They believe the best way to reduce income inequality is for individuals to take the initiative to improve their skills via education and effort.

## 27) **Free Markets and Global Competition**

Democrats oppose free markets and global competition because there are too many losers (lost American jobs) and too few winners.

Republicans support free markets and global competition because it increases our standard of living by creating better products and jobs.

## 28) **Free Trade Agreements**

Democrats oppose free trade agreements with other countries because they eliminate American jobs. However, they will support free trade agreements if American workers displaced by the agreement are assisted in finding new jobs.

Republicans support free trade agreements because they create new American jobs, open up new markets, and make it easier to trade with the other country or countries.

## 29) **Trade Deficits**

For almost 40 consecutive years the United States has imported more goods than it has exported. Money was borrowed to make up the difference, which has been over $500 billion a year in recent years. This makes the US the largest debtor nation. The US owes more money than countries owe the US.

The US owes more money to China than any other nation. Opponents say this huge discrepancy has eliminated millions of jobs, lowered the standard of living for the lower and middle class, and increased our national debt. Proponents say consumers are able to buy products at lower prices.

Democrats and Republicans are bipartisan on this issue because both support trade deficits. Even though these deficits add to the national debt, neither team has attempted to reverse the trend. Both teams are hoping the US can export more business services and new products to help correct this imbalance. Otherwise, don't expect these deficits to decrease anytime soon.

## 30) <u>Foreign Relations</u>

Democrats want other countries to like us and be friends with us. They believe we should listen, cooperate, and try not to upset them.

Republicans want other countries to respect us. They don't care what other countries think about us because they believe America's interests come first.

## 31) <u>United Nations</u>

Democrats support the United Nations and most of the decisions that are made there. They also believe that the United Nations should take the lead on international disputes.

Republicans believe the United Nations is anti-American,

anti-Semitic, incompetent, inefficient, corrupt, and wastes American taxpayer money.

## 32) <u>Israel / Palestine</u>

Democrats believe Israel should give up all occupied Palestinian land in return for peace.

Republicans believe Israel should give up occupied Palestinian land only after the Palestinians recognize Israel's right to exist as a free and sovereign nation.

## 33) <u>China</u>

Democrats and Republicans will both criticize China about monetary manipulation, trade deficits, human rights, democratic reform, counterfeit products, and patent infringements. But little, if anything, will change China's conduct.

## 34) <u>Defense / Military Spending</u>

Democrats want to decrease military spending. The US spends more on defense than any other country in the world. There aren't any major threats to our security, so money should be spent elsewhere.

Republicans want to increase military spending. They want the United States to be the strongest military power on earth. Plus, there is a huge military industry that provides American jobs.

## 35) Missile Defense

The United States is working to build a missile defense system that will shoot down missiles fired from enemy or rogue nations.

Democrats oppose a missile defense system because they believe it is too expensive to build and won't work. Plus, they don't believe any nation would be foolish to launch missiles at us.

Republicans support missile defense system because any nation with long-range missiles can attack us today. They believe that more unfriendly (and suicidal) nations will acquire long-range missiles and fire them at us some time in the future.

## 36) War

Democrats oppose war and believe it should only occur as a last resort. They believe diplomacy and economic/financial sanctions should be tried first. They also believe that the United States should never fight a war without other nations supporting our actions.

Republicans support the threat of war more than Democrats. They believe diplomacy and sanctions do not resolve issues, just prolong them. They don't care what other nations think about us or our war intentions. If it comes to war, Republicans have no problem with the United States conducting war without assistance from other countries.

## 37) Iranian Nuclear Deal

The United States and Iran made a deal that released $150 billion in frozen Iranian assets and delayed Iran's ability to build nuclear weapons.

Democrats support the Iranian Nuclear Deal because it made President Obama look good.

Republicans oppose the Iranian Nuclear Deal because Iran assists terrorists, it increases the likelihood that Iran's neighboring countries will also want to acquire nuclear weapons, and increases the chance of a nuclear war in that region.

## 38) Paying Ransom for Kidnapped Americans

Democrats support paying ransom to foreign countries in return of kidnapped Americans because they don't want the kidnapped American or their families to suffer.

Republicans oppose paying ransom because it will lead to more Americans being kidnapped.

## 39) Withdrawal of US Troops From Afghanistan

Democrats support the withdrawal of most US troops from Afghanistan regardless of what is happening there militarily.

Republicans support a flexible timeline to withdraw US troops from Afghanistan. They don't support a public deadline because the enemy will use this as an incentive for attacks after all our troops leave.

## 40) <u>Indefinite Detention of Terrorists Caught in US</u>

Democrats oppose the indefinite detention of terrorists caught inside the United States.

Republicans support the indefinite detention of terrorists caught inside the United States.

## 41) <u>Torture of Captured Terrorist</u>

Democrats oppose the torture of captured terrorists because they believe even terrorists should have personal rights, it violates international laws, and doesn't obtain useful information.

Republicans support the torture of captured terrorists because terrorists are not soldiers, useful information has been obtained, and it is worth it if just one innocent life is saved by the information obtained.

## 42) <u>Closing the Guantanamo Bay Detention Camp</u>

A few hundred dangerous combatants captured during the Afghanistan and Iraq wars have been held prisoner at this high-security facility within the Guantanamo Bay Naval Base in Cuba.

Democrats support closing the camp and either releasing the prisoners, transferring them to other countries, or sending them to a high-security prison inside the United States. They believe the camp is a recruiting tool for terrorists in the Middle East.

Republicans oppose closing the camp. They believe

these prisoners are too dangerous and should never be released. Over the years, many of the prisoners released by President Obama have returned to their terrorist activities and even killed Americans.

### 43) <u>Constitutional Rights for Captured Foreign Terrorist</u>

Democrats believe that captured foreign terrorists should be treated as American citizens and afforded all the protections under our Constitution.

Republicans believe captured foreign terrorists should not be protected by our Constitution because they are not American citizens.

### 44) <u>Military Veterans Benefits and VA Scandal</u>

During 2015 and 2016, corruption, fraud and mismanagement at the Veterans Administration (VA) prevented many military veterans from receiving the health care promised them by the government.

Both Democrats and Republicans have been guilty of neglecting military veterans over the past ten years. Both teams are developing solutions to improve the efficiency and oversight of the VA. It is expected that both teams will cooperate in solving this problem.

### 45) <u>Crime - Death Penalty</u>

Democrats oppose the death penalty. They are very concerned that an innocent person will be executed. Many consider it cruel and unusual punishment. Nor do they believe it prevents others from committing future crimes. They would prefer to keep the most violent criminals in prison for the rest of their life regardless of the cost to taxpayers.

Republicans support the death penalty. In fact, they don't believe it happens fast and often enough. Many believe it is the right thing to do when serious crimes have been committed. Republicans oppose keeping those sentenced to death in prison for life because it's expensive to incarcerate keep and most criminals will be released back into society eventually.

## 46) Crime - Overcrowded Prisons

Democrats support the early release of non-violent prisoners to alleviate prison overcrowding. They don't support building additional prisons because that money could be used to prevent crimes in the first place.

Republicans support building more prisons, if necessary, to ensure our most violent criminals are off the streets. They also believe that prisoners should serve their full sentences and prisons should be a nasty place that criminals want to avoid.

## 47) Crime - Rehabilitation

Democrats support rehabilitating criminals while in prison because without rehabilitation the criminal is likely to commit crime again.

Republicans seem to believe that the best approach is to

lock up criminals and throw away the key until they have served their complete sentence. They believe rehabilitating criminals is a waste of taxpayer money because they haven't seen a majority of positive results.

### 48) <u>Crime - Racial, Ethnic, and Religious Profiling</u>

Democrats oppose law enforcement personnel from using racial, ethnic, and religious profiling because it is an illegal form of discrimination and a violation of one's civil rights.

Republicans support the use of racial, ethnic, and religious profiling by law enforcement personnel because it is necessary to keep the country safe and has already prevented future terrorist attacks within the United States.

### 49) <u>Police Body Cameras</u>

Democrats believe all police officers should be forced to wear and activate body cameras. They believe that if every action by a police officer is recorded, they are more accountable for their actions, less abuse of criminals would occur, and are useful as evidence at criminal trials.

Republicans believe each police department should determine if and who should wear a camera. Privacy issues and the ability of an officer act instinctively are also concerns with wearing a camera.

### 50) <u>Stand-Your-Ground Law</u>

This law (in some states) allows one to use physical or

lethal force to defend their life if they feel threatened wherever they may be.

Democrats oppose the Stand-Your-Ground law because innocent people could be hurt or killed. Plus, no one should be able to take the law into their own hands.

Republicans support the Stand-Your-Ground law because they believe everyone has the right to defend their life wherever and whenever they believe their life is threatened.

## 51) <u>Affirmative Action</u>

This is a policy used to hire employees or admit students into schools based on their race, skin color, gender, sexual orientation, and religion. In the past, people were discriminated against because of these characteristics. Affirmative action is used to correct discrimination against minorities or underrepresented people. It is controversial because many believe less qualified people are hired or admitted into schools.

Democrats support affirmative action. They believe businesses and schools should be forced to hire less qualified applicants that are underrepresented. They believe discrimination still exists in the workplace and school admissions. Affirmative action lessens that discrimination.

Republicans oppose affirmative action. They believe businesses and schools should be able to select the most qualified, talented, and hard-working people they can find. Their attitude is winning sports teams don't implement affirmative action, so neither should schools and businesses that want to be successful.

## 52) <u>Abortion</u>

Abortion is a form of birth control where a woman's pregnancy is deliberately terminated. The United States Supreme Court legalized abortion in 1973.

Democrats support a woman's right to terminate her pregnancy because a woman should have complete control over her body and health.

Republicans believe abortion is murder because innocent and helpless life is deliberately terminated.

## 53) <u>Health Care - ObamaCare</u>

ObamaCare is the name given to the Patient Protection and Affordable Care Act (ACA) passed by President Obama and his fellow Democrats. ObamaCare provides access to health care for all Americans. Every Republican voted against the law.

Democrats passed this law because millions of Americans do not have access to health care.

Republicans believe this law will create a new and huge government bureaucracy that will be more costly, less efficient, and decide who can receive specific care and when that care will be provided. They believe a market-based health care system would be better.

## 54) ObamaCare – Repealing the Law

Democrats are in favor of fixing, not repealing or replacing, ObamaCare.

Republicans are in favor of repealing and replacing ObamaCare with a market-driven health care program.

## 55) ObamaCare - Individual Mandate

One aspect of ObamaCare is that every American must purchase health insurance. If they don't, they will be fined. Many young and healthy people don't purchase health insurance.

Democrats support this mandate because in order to keep health care affordable for everybody and costs down, everyone, especially healthy people, must purchase health insurance.

Republicans don't support this issue because the government should not be allowed to force anyone to purchase something they don't want to buy.

## 56) ObamaCare - Employers Must Cover Contraception

Another aspect of ObamaCare is that all employers must cover birth control or contraceptives for their employees. Many religious hospitals and schools oppose birth control and contraceptives. They believe they should be exempt from this mandate.

Democrats don't believe religious hospitals or schools should receive an exemption because this is a health issue not a religious issue.

Republicans believe religious hospitals or schools should be exempt because providing contraceptives goes against a fundamental belief of these institutions.

### 57) Health Care - Obesity

Democrats believe the government should play a major role in reducing the staggering increase in obesity because obesity increases health care costs.

Republicans believe that obesity is a personal freedom and shouldn't be of any concern to the government, and any attempt to legislate obesity would be a waste of taxpayer money.

### 58) School Meal Nutritional Standards

These standards determine what foods can be served at meals in public schools. The purpose was to assist in decreasing obesity in children by providing healthier meals.

Democrats support government telling public schools what children can and cannot eat at meals served inside schools.

Republicans don't support the standards because the kids are not eating the healthier meals and obesity isn't decreasing.

### 59) Health Care - Euthanasia or Assisted Suicide

Euthanasia is the act of painlessly killing a medical patient that is in pain and has a terminal disease or ailment.

Democrats support euthanasia because a person should have the right to end their life when they want to.

Republicans oppose euthanasia because they respect life.

## 60) Health Care - Medicinal Marijuana

Democrats support legalizing medicinal marijuana usage to reduce severe pain experienced by medical patients. They also believe it should be prescribed by a physician, regulated, and supervised by the government.

Republicans oppose legalizing medicinal marijuana because it is an illegal drug and other legal drugs can be used to reduce severe pain experienced by medical patients. They also believe legalizing medicinal marijuana will lead to legalizing recreational marijuana.

## 61) Legalized Marijuana and Other Drugs

A few states have made it legal to purchase marijuana for personal recreational use.

Democrats believe the war on marijuana and other illegal drugs has been a waste of time and government resources, and the criminal punishment is too harsh. Many Democrats support legalizing illegal drugs. Numerous countries have legalized drugs without major negative affect.

Republicans believe the war on illegal drugs should continue and tougher punishments handed out. They oppose legalizing illegal drugs because they will threaten public and personal safety.

## 62) <u>Medical Research and Animal Rights</u>

Democrats believe medical research that uses animals is cruel and inhumane. Alternative ways should be found to advance medicine research without using animals.

Republicans believe animals should be treated as humanely as possible. But when it comes to choosing between advancing medicine by making animals suffer in order to improve the lives of humans, humans take priority over animal rights.

## 63) <u>Imported Oil</u>

Democrats believe that our dependency on imported oil should decrease and public investments in alternative energy sources, such as wind and solar power, should increase.

Republicans support decreasing our dependency on imported oil but only if the technology for alternative energy sources makes it cheaper and more efficient than oil.

## 64) <u>Environment</u>

Democrats favor protecting the environment at all costs.

Republicans believe most environmental costs are unnecessary and place a financial burden on businesses and people.

## 65) <u>Environment - Global Warming and Climate Change</u>

Democrats believe global warming and climate change is

caused by automobiles emissions and industrial pollution released into the air.

Most Republicans believe global warming and climate change has not been proven definitively.

## 66) Environment - Keystone Pipeline

The Keystone pipeline is a proposed oil pipeline from Canadian oil fields to Nebraska.

Democrats oppose the pipeline because it would be installed near underground water, which could become contaminated if the pipeline broke.

Republicans support building the pipeline because they believe safety measures will ensure that the underground water will be protected.

## 67) Environment - Hydraulic Fracturing

Hydraulic fracturing or "fracking" is a drilling technique that uses high-pressure liquid to crack open underground rock in order to reach oil or natural gas.

Democrats oppose hydraulic fracking because of the risk of contaminating underground water and the possibility of causing earthquakes where the fracking occurs.

Republicans support hydraulic fracking because they believe the technique is safe and will not contaminate underground water.

## 68) Environment - ANWR Oil Exploration

The Arctic National Wildlife Refuge (ANWR) is a 19-million acre protected wildlife area in northern Alaska. ANWR is inhabited by arctic wildlife and a small population of humans.

Democrats oppose ANWR oil exploration because they don't believe there is much oil in the ground and drilling would disrupt the wildlife habitat.

Republicans believe we need to reduce our dependence on oil imports. Drilling for ANWR oil would help. Only 1.5 million of the 19 million acres would be drilled upon. And new drilling techniques would minimize wildlife habitat disturbance.

## 69) Environment - Oil and Natural Gas Exploration

Democrats believe alternative sources of energy need to be discovered instead of exploring for oil and natural gas. Overall, they oppose oil and natural gas exploration because of potential wildlife disruptions and air and underground pollution.

Republicans support oil and gas exploration because it will be many years before alternative energy sources become abundant, efficient, and affordable.

## 70) Environment - Offshore Oil Exploration

Democrats oppose offshore oil exploration and drilling because of potential spills and the affect the oil has on wildlife, marine life and beaches.

Republicans support offshore oil exploration to reduce

the need of buying oil from other countries. Plus, they believe proper safety techniques, when followed, prevent oil spills.

## 71) Environment - Coal Industry

Democrats want to shutdown the coal industry because of the air pollution emitted when coal is burned by electricity-producing power plants. Plus, the extraction process is dangerous for coal miners and scars the land.

Republicans support the coal industry because coal is an abundant resource within the United States and is one of the main sources used to create electricity today.

## 72) Environment - Nuclear Energy and New Plants

Democrats oppose nuclear energy and the building of new nuclear plants because of the potential for a nuclear meltdown or an accident that releases radioactive material into the air.

Republicans support nuclear energy and the building of new plants because the demand for electricity continues to grow and nuclear is the most efficient way to create electricity.

## 73) Environment - Disposal of Radioactive Waste

Nuclear plants generate radioactive waste. That waste has been stored at nuclear plant sites for years. The plants are running out of storage space.

Democrats support keeping the waste at the nuclear plant

sites. They believe storing the waste off site could leak and contaminate ground and water.

Republicans support moving and burying nuclear waste deep under a mountain in Nevada. They believe it will stay safe and not pollute nearby water or ground.

## 74) <u>Environment - Wind Energy</u>

Democrats support wind energy because it is plentiful, doesn't pollute, and is an alternative energy source to oil and natural gas.

Republicans oppose wind energy because it is not efficient, takes up a lot of space, and currently doesn't generate much electricity.

## 75) <u>Environment - Solar Energy</u>

Democrats support solar energy because the sun is always on, doesn't pollute, and is an alternative energy source.

Republicans oppose solar energy because it is too expensive, doesn't work on cloudy days or at night, and currently doesn't generate much electricity.

## 76) <u>Water For Humans Or Endangered Species</u>

There have been numerous incidents where access to water between humans and endangered species was debated.

Democrats support water for endangered species over human usage.

Republicans support water for human usage over endangered species.

## 77) <u>CAFE Mileage Standards</u>

The Corporate Average Fuel Economy (CAFE) determines how many miles per gallon of gas automobiles should reach by a specific date.

Democrats support higher EPA mileage standards because since less gasoline is used, the amount of oil needed to be imported decreases. Plus, there's less air pollution.

Republicans oppose higher EPA mileage standards because it increases research and development costs on automobile manufacturers. Plus, the new standards will make the resulting cars more expensive, smaller, and less safe.

## 78) <u>Wall Street Oil Speculators (Oil Futures)</u>

Oil futures or oil speculation is an investment where a specific amount of oil is purchased at a specific price, then held onto. Because the oil is held and not released into the market, there is an artificial shortage that causes the price of oil to increase. And when the price of oil increases, so does the price of gasoline and heating oil.

Democrats oppose Wall Street oil speculators and believe it should be outlawed or restricted because it doesn't serve any purpose but to artificially increase the price of heating oil and gasoline for everyone.

Republicans support oil speculators because it is another type of investment. And oil speculators can and do lose money.

## 79) Education - Funding

Democrats support increased funding for education with minimal accountability to the taxpayers.

Republicans support less funding for education unless there is more accountability to the taxpayer.

## 80) Education - Head Start

Head Start is a government program that provides preschool educational services to children of low-income families.

Democrats support Head Start because many low-income parents must work and cannot be home to provide preschool education for their children.

Republicans oppose Head Start because a lot of tax dollars have been spent on this program and very little benefit to children has been identified.

## 81) Education - Ineffective Teachers

Democrats protect ineffective public school teachers. Most public teachers belong to labor unions, which support Democrats.

Republicans support removing ineffective teachers from schools as quickly as possible.

## 82) Education - No Child Left Behind

No Child Left Behind is a federal law that tests public school students from grade 3 through grade 12 in science, reading, and math to determine if they have met minimum learning standards. If the test scores do not meet the goals, schools can be closed and teachers and administrators can be fired. Since billions of dollars a year are spent on public education, this bills attempts to make schools accountable for the money they receive.

Democrats and Republicans both want to reform this complex law but there is no consensus among the teams as to how to improve it or whether to eliminate it.

## 83) Education - School Vouchers

A school voucher is where taxpayer money is given to parents so they can send their children to private or charter schools.

Democrats oppose school vouchers because the money could be used to improve public schools.

Republicans support school vouchers because they believe students get better educated and disciplined in private or charter schools compared to public schools.

## 84) Education - Charter Schools

A charter school is a grade or high school that is intended to be a more efficient alternative to public schools. Charter schools compete for students and public funding.

Democrats oppose charter schools because less public money goes to public schools and their teachers.

Republicans support charter schools because they believe competition for students and public funding forces public schools to improve teaching and test score results.

### 85) Education - College Student Loans

Bankruptcy laws do not allow college students loans to be forgiven. Those loans must be repaid. Collectively, students owe over $1 trillion in student loans. And many students are having difficulty repaying their loans.

Democrats support changing the bankruptcy laws to allow students to have their loans forgiven. They also support forgiving student loans after a specific number of years.

Republicans oppose changing the bankruptcy laws because federal and private loans would become more risky for the bank or government and thus more expensive and difficult to obtain for the student.

### 86) Education - In-State Tuition for Illegal Immigrants

College students that go to a college or university in their home state pay much less than students from another state.

Democrats support allowing illegal immigrants to pay in-state tuition because it makes college more affordable.

Republicans oppose allowing illegal immigrants to pay in-state tuition because with classroom space limited, legal students should be given priority over illegal students. Plus, it is not fair to those legal students from other states to pay higher tuition than a student that is an illegal immigrant.

## 87) Education – Common Core Curriculum

Common core curriculum is a set of national education standards used to identify what will be taught to all public school students from kindergarten through high school.

Democrats support common core curriculum because there is a consistent curriculum taught among all public schools.

Republicans oppose common core curriculum because they believe state and local schools should have control over what is taught to their students.

## 88) Education - Bilingualism

Bilingualism is where public schools teach students from another country to learn in their native language (mostly Spanish) in addition to teaching them in English.

Democrats support bilingualism in schools because it helps the student feel inclusive in the school and believe the student will learn English at a faster pace. Democrats believe it is discrimination to force a student to learn English.

Republicans oppose bilingualism in schools because it is costly to hire teaches and buy learning material for multiple languages. Forcing students to learn only English helps them assimilate faster into the mainstream culture. And most employers require employees to speak English.

## 89) English - America's Official Language

This issue is mainly a symbolic issue. Laws, safety, and health information are communicated in languages other than English due to the growing number of non-English speaking citizens.

Democrats believe that there should be no official language in the United States. They don't want to offend non-English speaking citizens.

Republicans believe that English should be written into law as the official language of the United States.

## 90) Social Security Reform

Democrats and Republicans won't offer any major changes in Social Security unless one team wins complete control of the government.

If Democrats won complete control of government, they would raise payroll taxes on higher wage earners to keep Social Security solvent. They would prohibit privatization or investment of Social Security funds in the stock or bond markets. They would reduce or eliminate Social Security benefits to wealthy Americans by evaluating their finances by using a means test.

If Republicans won complete control of government, they would raise the eligibility age for Social Security, but not for current benefit recipients. They would also allow all wage earners to invest some of their Social Security funds in the stock and bond markets in order to obtain a higher rate of return compared to Social Security's rate of return.

## 91) Welfare Reform

Welfare is a government program that provides financial, food, and housing assistance to Americans.

Democrats oppose welfare reform because the reforms would reduce benefits and hurt recipients, especially in this stagnant economy. They would raise taxes on wealthy Americans to pay for the rising cost of welfare.

Republicans support welfare reform because they believe that welfare recipients become too dependent on it. Plus, welfare costs are increasing rapidly, and cutting welfare spending is better than raising taxes to pay for it.

## 92) Medicare / Medicaid Reform

Medicare is a national health care plan for Americans 65 years and older. Medicaid is a health care plan for low-income Americans.

Democrats oppose Medicare/Medicaid reform because the reforms would reduce benefits and hurt recipients, especially in this stagnant economy. They would raise taxes on wealthy

Americans to pay for the increasing cost of Medicare/Medicaid.

Republicans support reducing Medicare/Medicaid spending and eliminating waste, fraud, and abuse while introducing market competition. They believe changes must be made because the cost of Medicare/Medicaid in the future is expected to skyrocket and run out of funding sooner than estimated.

### 93) Super PACS and Campaign Finance Reform

Super PACs (Political Action Committees) are groups that raise huge amounts of money that are spent on political candidates or causes. The money comes from unions, organizations, groups, corporations, or individuals. There is no limit on the amount of money that can be raised.

Here is another bipartisan issue both Democrats and Republicans support. Each side believes it can and must raise more money than the other in order to get their political messages communicated to the voters. Thus, any discussion about campaign finance reform is now dead until political corruption or major abuses are discovered.

### 94) Federal Jobs Training Program

Democrats support federal jobs training programs because it gives the public the impression that government is trying to assist the unemployed in finding a job.

Republicans oppose federal jobs training programs

because they are ineffective and generate too much inefficiency, waste, fraud, and abuse. They believe money for jobs training should be given to the states to administer.

## 95) <u>The Constitution</u>

Democrats believe the Constitution is a flexible document that should be interpreted based on the current societal attitude towards laws, morals, and the direction of the country.

Republicans believe the Constitution is a rigid document that should be interpreted based on what the original authors intended, not on how society currently feels about law, morals, and the direction of the country.

## 96) <u>Judicial Activism</u>

Judicial Activism is where judges disregard current law and make decisions based on their personal opinion.

Democrats support judicial activism because public opinion can change over time.

Republicans oppose judicial activism because it disregards or overrides current laws that passed through the law-making process.

## 97) <u>Supreme Court Justices</u>

Democrats believe Supreme Court Justices should make policy based on their own interpretation of the laws and public opinion.

Republicans believe Supreme Court Justices should make decisions based on the Constitution, not their personal beliefs.

## 98) <u>Tort (Legal) Reform</u>

Tort reform would place a monetary limit on how much litigants could receive if they won a lawsuit.

Democrats oppose tort reform because lawyers are large financial contributors to Democrats.

Republicans support tort reform because they believe many jury awards are outrageous and increase business expenses.

## 99) <u>Gun Control (2<sup>nd</sup> Amendment)</u>

Democrats support gun control laws that restrict gun ownership and types of guns and ammunition sold because guns lead to unnecessary violence.

Republicans oppose gun control laws because everyone should have the right to possess guns to protect themselves and their families. Plus, gun possession is the only thing that prevents big government from completely controlling our lives.

## 100) <u>Government Spying On US Citizens</u>

Both Democrats and Republicans believe the government should continue spying on American citizens in order to keep society safe from terrorist attacks.

**101)**   <u>**Tea Party**</u>

The Tea Party is the name of a political movement that protests wasteful government spending.

Democrats oppose the Tea Party because they support big government spending.

Republicans support the Tea Party because they believe there is a lot of wasteful government spending that should be eliminated.

**102)**   <u>**IRS Targeting Conservatives**</u>

The Internal Revenue Service (IRS), under a Democrat president, was caught harassing non-profit conservative political groups for political purposes.  The political groups were targeted because they were raising large amounts of tax-free money to be used to support Republican candidates and causes.

Democrats supported this activity because it would prevent these conservative groups from obtaining non-profit status and tax-free money.

Republicans opposed the IRS's targeting of conservative groups because the IRS should not deliberately target people or groups for political purposes.

**103)**   <u>**Occupy Wall Street**</u>

Occupy Wall Street is the name of a political movement that protests the inequities of capitalism, Wall Street's influence on government, and the economic turmoil that affected many

Americans after the government bailed out large Wall Street banks and firms.

Democrats support the Occupy Wall Street movement because Democrats want to be seen as assisting ordinary citizens and standing up to Wall Street.

Republicans oppose the Occupy Wall Street movement because the bailouts were necessary and Wall Street is vital to the economy of the United States.

## 104)  <u>Infrastructure</u>

Infrastructure refers to maintaining or building new public schools, roads, bridges, highways, sewers, and power grids.

Democrats support giving more funding for infrastructure projects because it creates good-paying union jobs. And labor unions overwhelmingly vote for Democrats.

Republicans oppose giving more funding for infrastructure because they believe many of these projects are temporary, costly, and wasteful.

## 105)  <u>High-Speed Railways</u>

Democrats support building high-speed railways because it creates union construction jobs and reduces air pollution.

Republicans oppose building high-speed railways because they are very expensive to build and maintain. Plus, there are other modes of transportation available.

## 106) <u>God and Religion</u>

Democrats believe God and religion is a private matter that should be removed from government.

Republicans believe God and religion were two of the important foundations our country was founded on and should play a visible role in government.

## 107) <u>Prayer in Public Schools</u>

Democrats oppose any praying on public school property. They believe prayer is a private matter.

Republicans support praying on public school property because praying is a freedom of speech.

## 108) <u>Moral Authority</u>

Democrats believe more and more that there is no moral authority as to what is right and wrong. They increasingly believe that each individual can live and act as they choose regardless of traditional societal norms and values.

Republicans still believe that God and God's word passed down through the centuries is the guiding moral authority in how we live and act.

## 109) <u>The Origin of Life and Evolution</u>

Democrats believe life originated from the Big Bang theory, and life on earth evolved through evolution.

Republicans believe that God created the heavens, earth, and all life on earth. Plus, evolution of species occurs on earth but originates from God.

## 110) <u>Same-Sex or Gay Marriage</u>

Same-sex or gay marriage is marriage between a man and another man, or a woman and another woman. Once married, they would enjoy all of the legal rights of a traditional (man and woman) marriage.

Democrats support gay marriage because they believe it is a civil right that should be available to all Americans regardless of their sexual orientation.

Republicans oppose gay marriage because it is morally and religiously wrong. They believe that marriage should only occur between a man and a woman.

## 111) <u>Discrimination and Religious Freedom</u>

Some states allow individuals and businesses to discriminate based on their religious beliefs.

Democrats oppose any discrimination based on religious beliefs.

Republicans support discrimination based on religious beliefs. For example, they believe it's okay for a bakery not to make a cake for a gay wedding if gay marriage is against the religious beliefs of the owner of the bakery.

## 112)   Transgenders and Bathroom Usage

Many states are wrestling with which public bathroom transgender individuals can be allowed to use. There are basically two sides. One side says that if a transgender was born a male, the transgender must use the male bathroom. The second side says that if a transgender was born a male but identifies as a female, the transgender can use the female bathroom. There's a safety concern of men using women's bathrooms. Others contend it's a personal choice issue.

Democrats support transgender individuals using the bathroom they identify with.

Republicans support transgender individuals using the bathroom of the sex they were born.

## 113)   Politically Correct Language

Politically correct language is any language that doesn't offend someone.

Democrats support politically correct language. They believe that no one should feel offended by written or spoken words.

Republicans oppose politically correct language. They believe that it restricts freedom of speech and that no one should have authority over what is written or spoken.

## 114)   Gender-Neutral Language

Gender neutral language eliminates any identifier of sex,

such as the elimination of the words "he" and "she."

Democrats support gender neutral language. They believe people can feel excluded if a specific gender is described.

Republicans oppose gender neutral language. They believe it is another political correct attack on traditional values.

### 115)  Washington Redskins Name

The Washington Redskins is a professional football team in Washington, D.C.  There is debate concerning whether the name 'Redskins' is a derogatory term to Native Americans.  The team was named 'Redskins' in 1932.  Only recently has the name been criticized.

Democrats believe the name is a derogatory term and should be replaced with another name.

Republicans believe the name is a term of honor and respect and should not be replaced.

### 116)  Black Lives Matter

Is a movement that attempts to prevent violence and racism against black Americans.

Democrats support black lives matter because most black voters vote for Democrats.

Republicans oppose black lives matter because they believe all lives matter, regardless of skin color.

## 117) Screening Refugees for Terrorist

President Obama wants to import refugees from countries that also have numerous terrors living there. Currently, there is not much the government can do to ensure that there are no terrorists among the refugees entering the country.

Democrats support allowing refugees into the country regardless if terrorists are among them. They believe that these refugees will eventually vote for Democrat politicians.

Republicans support the thorough screening of every refugee before they can enter the United States. This is to ensure that terrorists do not enter and the American public is kept safe.

## 118) Illegal Immigration and Amnesty

Democrats support illegal immigration. They also support amnesty or a path to citizenship for those already in the United States.

Republicans oppose illegal immigration because no one should ever be rewarded for breaking our laws. Plus, illegal immigration increases crime, the cost of education and health care. They oppose amnesty.

## 119) Illegal Immigration - Secured US/Mexican Border

Democrats support an open US/Mexican border where illegal immigrants can enter the United States without being stopped and returned.

Republicans support a closed and secure US/Mexican

border to prevent illegal immigrants from entering.

## 120)    Illegal Immigration – Deportation of Children

Over the last few years, thousands of illegal immigrant children entered the United States by themselves.

Democrats don't want to deport any illegal immigrants, be they children or adults. They believe a majority of illegal immigrants will always be dependent on government for financial assistance and will vote for Democrat politicians if they become citizens.

Republicans support the deportation of all illegal immigrants. They oppose efforts to make them citizens because they also believe they will vote for Democrats and depend on the government for financial assistance.

## 121)    Illegal Immigration – Sanctuary Cities

Sanctuary cities are cities that will not cooperate with the government to hold illegal immigrants so that they can eventually be deported.

Democrats thoroughly support sanctuary cities. They believe that the longer illegal immigrants are allowed to stay in the country, the sooner they will become citizens and eventually vote for Democrat politicians.

Republicans thoroughly condemn sanctuary cities and find it appalling that cities would deliberately work against the government to prevent illegal immigrants from eventually being deported.

## 122)   **Illegal Immigration - Dream Act**

The Dream Act is a proposal to allow illegal immigrants to live legally within the United States and eventually become a US citizen.

Democrats support the Dream Act because they believe most immigrant voters support the act and will vote for the team that supports it.

Republicans oppose the Dream Act because they believe it rewards lawbreakers and encourages more illegal immigrants to enter the United States.

## 123)   **H-1B Visas**

H-1B visas are visas given to a maximum of 65,000 foreign workers each year that allow them to enter and work in the United States. Many companies claim they need to hire these special foreign workers because they cannot find qualified American workers. Critics say companies hire foreign workers because they usually work for less compensation than an American worker.

Democrats and Republicans are not consistently for or against raising the number of H-1B visas given out annually. Where high-tech jobs are located, most politicians support raising the quota because most H-1B visas are given to highly skilled and educated foreign workers. Where unemployment is high, politicians usually favor either eliminating giving H-1B visas entirely, lowering or keeping the quota at it's current level. You'll have to do research as to the position of your local, state and national candidates stand.

### 124)   Labor Unions and The Right To Work

Right-to-work is a concept that believes a person has the right to work without being forced to join a labor union. Currently, 26 states have right-to-work laws.

Democrats oppose right-to-work laws because they believe it restricts the creation or growth of labor unions. Plus, labor union members overwhelmingly vote for Democrats.

Republicans support right-to-work laws because businesses don't like negotiating with labor unions. And labor unions increase business expenses. Plus, businesses have more flexibility with employees that are not unionized.

### 125)   Union Card Check

Card check is a unionizing technique where employees vote for or against unionizing using a non-secret or open ballot.

Democrats love card checks because union leaders can personally encourage workers to sign a union pledge ballot.

Republicans oppose card checks because of the potential for employee coercion by union representatives. They support secret ballot voting, even though most Republicans oppose unions entirely.

## 126)  <u>Collective Bargaining Rights for Public Employees</u>

In some states, the rights of government (public) employees to collective bargain is being eliminated or severely restricted, forcing those government employees to financially contribute more towards their health care insurance and pension plans. These states are doing this to decrease state spending and assist in balancing their state budgets, while transferring those costs to the government workers. Normally the taxpayers would pay these government perks.

Democrats oppose the elimination of collective bargaining rights for government employees because these employees are mostly unionized, vote for Democrats, and earned these rights, benefits, and wages through collective bargaining agreements that they insist should be honored.

Republicans support the elimination of collective bargaining rights for government employees because these agreements were negotiated years ago under more favorable economic times, were too generous to the employees, and cannot be paid for without drastically raising taxes or filing for bankruptcy. They also believe the employees should pay more for their benefits to lessen the taxpayer burden. And eliminating collective bargain rights will make it easier for states to balance their budgets.

## 127)  <u>Voter Identification (I.D.)</u>

Democrats oppose requiring voters provide valid

identification in order to vote on Election Day because it would prevent those without an ID card from voting in person.

Republicans support requiring voters provide valid identification in order to vote on Election Day because everyone should already have an ID card if they drive a car or have an account at a bank. Plus, showing a valid ID would reduce voter fraud.

### 128) <u>Voting Rights for Convicted Felons</u>

Each state determines if convicted felons in their state are allowed to vote.

Democrats support allowing convicted felons to vote because most felons are registered Democrats or lean voting for Democrats.

Republicans oppose allowing convicted felons to vote unless specific requirements are met by the felon.

### 129) <u>Big City Bailouts</u>

By law, cities must balance their budget, which means they cannot spend more money than they bring in. Many American cities are having difficulty balancing their budgets and may ask the federal government for financial assistance. Cities can cut government services (like police and fire protection), raise taxes, do both, or file for bankruptcy to protect them from long-term financial obligations, such as government employee pensions.

Democrats support federal bailout of cities in financial distress because the cities don't have the tax base to raise taxes, have already cut as much spending as possible, and don't want to see city union employee wages and pensions reduced. Union employees usually vote for Democrats, and most cities asking for bailouts are governed by Democrats.

Republicans oppose any federal bailout because they believe the cities brought these problems on themselves, saw the problems coming, and failed to take necessary action well in advance. Plus, they support cities filing for bankruptcy because then that city's state can take over the city and void labor and pension contracts with city workers in order to balance their budgets.

**130)  Extending Unemployment Benefits**

Democrats support extending unemployment benefits indefinitely.

Republicans oppose extending unemployment benefits because the recipients become too dependent on the government and don't look for employment. They support giving former employees a hand up, not a long-term handout.

**131)  Regulations**

Democrats support regulations because they believe the government knows what is best for society.

Republicans oppose regulations because they believe it

increases business costs and restricts business growth.

## 132) <u>Size of Government</u>

Democrats support as big a government as possible. They believe the government, not the private sector, can improve the lives of Americans.

Republicans support as small a government as possible. They believe the private sector, not big government, can improve the lives of Americans.

## 133) <u>Presidential Recess Appointments</u>

The president has the authority to appoint officials to top government posts without Senate approval when the Senate is not in session.

Democrats currently support presidential recess appointments because the president is a Democrat and want the president's nominee, who's likely to be a Democrat, to be approved.

Republicans currently oppose presidential recess appointments because the president is a Democrat and many times do not approve of the nominated official.

## 134) <u>Socialism</u>

Socialism is where the government decides what is best for you, instead of you deciding what is best for you!

Democrats support socialism more than Republicans

because people are selfish and will attempt to make their life better at the expense of others. And government needs to police these selfish actions.

Republicans oppose socialism more than Democrats because the Declaration of Independence gives everyone the right to life, liberty, and the pursuit of happiness.

## 135)   Space Exploration

Democrats oppose funding for space exploration because there are other more pressing social issues to be funded.

Republicans support private industry pursuing space exploration with minimal government funding.

## 136)   Public Broadcasting

Democrats support taxpayer funding of public broadcasting because it is educational and available to all Americans that don't have cable or satellite TV.

Republicans oppose taxpayer funding of public broadcasting because public broadcasting earns enough money without public funding. They believe public broadcasting is a form of entertainment, and the government shouldn't be in the entertainment business. Plus, they believe many of the programs are biased toward the Democrats' views.

## 137)   Internet Piracy

Democrats and Republicans want to stop internet piracy

of movies and music. But the laws they proposed might restrict internet users too much. So both teams have backed off this issue for now.

## 138)   Out-of-Wedlock Births

Democrats support out-of-wedlock births because they believe many of these mothers and their children will require government assistance in order to survive in an every increasing challenging world. And because they are getting government assistance, they believe these mothers will vote for Democrats.

Republicans oppose out-of-wedlock births because it breaks up families, speeds up the social deterioration of our society, and increases government spending.

## 139)   Paycheck Fairness Act

The Paycheck Fairness Act is a bill in Congress that if passed would force businesses to pay women the same wage as a man for the same amount of work. The authors of the bill believe wage discrimination is occurring against some women in the workforce.

Democrats support the bill because businesses should treat all their employees the same regardless of skill, education, experience, responsibilities, effort, and how profitable they make the business. In other words, all employees should be treated as if they are all in a labor union, where everybody earns the same wage or performing the same job tasks.

Republicans oppose this bill because the government shouldn't be forcing businesses what to pay their employees. Not all employees are created equal, even if they do the same job. Pay should be determined by businesses, not government, based on the hard work and talent an individual provides. Plus, they believe this law would increase paperwork and pay-related lawsuits against businesses.

## 140)  <u>War On Women</u>

War on women is a campaign slogan Democrats use to criticize Republicans, mainly on women reproduction and equal pay issues.

Democrats believe Republicans are conducting a war on women because Democrats believe there should be no restrictions on abortion and a woman should have complete say on reproduction issues.

Republicans believe the war on women is a slick marketing phrase being used by Democrats in an attempt to demonize Republican positions on abortion, the right to life, and equal pay issues.

## 141)  <u>Give the People What They Want</u>

Democrats support giving the people what they want regardless of the cost. They believe this prevents social unrest.

Republicans oppose giving what the people want because we don't have the money and resources to meet all the wants of the people.

## 142)   <u>The American Dream</u>

The American Dream is a belief that through hard work and talent any American can reach their highest personal potential, be successful, and prosper.

Democrats believe the American Dream is still accessible to all Americans but is getting more difficult because of inequities in our society. However, they believe government has to play a larger role in assisting more Americans in reaching their goals.

Republicans believe the American Dream is still accessible to all Americans but is getting more difficult due to government interference. However, they believe more Americans could reach it sooner if our government was smaller, more efficient, less restrictive, and more supportive of businesses.

## 143)   <u>Are You Better Off Today Than Two Years Ago?</u>

Since Democrat Barack Obama is president, whether Americans are better off or worse today compared to two years ago is usually attributed to the president. Thus, Democrats will argue Americans are better off, while Republicans will argue Americans are worse off.

Democrats believe Americans are BETTER off today than two years ago because:

- There are more green jobs and green industries.
- Air pollution has decreased.
- Overall inflation has decreased.
- Government annual deficits have decreased.
- The home foreclosure rate has decreased.
- ObamaCare has provided care to millions of Americans.
- Banks are less likely to fail.
- Mortgage interest rates are near their all time lows.
- Auto manufacturers are building more cars and adding jobs.
- The Dow Jones and NASDAQ stock markets are up.
- Corporate profits have increased.
- Worker and manufacturing productivity has increased.
- Foreign oil imports have decreased.
- Domestic oil exports have increased.
- Domestic oil discovery and production has greatly increased.
- Auto accident fatalities have decreased.
- The average price of a gallon of gasoline has decreased.
- Cancer deaths have decreased.
- Overall crime is down.
- The cost of electronic goods has decreased.
- Acceptance of homosexuality is up.
- Overall discrimination is down.
- Our society is much more diverse and inclusive.

Republicans believe Americans are WORSE off today than two years ago because:

- Overall government spending has skyrocketed.
- Government debt has increased by trillions of dollars.
- Many states have been forced to raise taxes to balance their budgets.
- Overall imports of material and products exceed exports.
- The cost of college has increased.
- The cost of food has increased.
- Household credit card debt has increased.
- Job growth has decreased.
- Millions of Americans have given up looking for work.

- There are more permanently unemployed Americans.
- There are fewer employees in the labor market.
- The poverty rate has skyrocketed.
- Births to unwedded mothers have increased.
- There are more people on welfare, food stamps and disability.
- Health, auto, and home insurance rates have increased.
- ObamaCare insurance premiums have increased.
- Local, state, and federal taxes are higher.
- Utility bills have increased.
- Interest rates for certificates of deposits (CDs) have decreased.
- Americans on fixed incomes have less disposable money.
- Net worth of Americans has decreased.
- Workers' wages have stagnated or decreased.
- Americans are working more hours and multiple jobs.
- More Americans cannot afford to retire.
- More lottery tickets have been bought.
- Depression has increased.
- Opiate dependency has increased.
- Inner city murders have increased.
- Murder/suicides have increased.
- Mass murders have increased.
- Radical Islamic terror attacks and murder have increased.
- More Americans bought a gun for personal protection.
- America is more divided politically and racially than ever.
- A majority of Americans believe the country is headed in the wrong direction.

***This book will continue…in 2018!***